From Concept to Completion: A Dissertation-Writing Guide for History Students

by the **AHA Graduate and Early Career Committee**

with essays by **Leora Auslander, W. Fitzhugh Brundage, Anthony Grafton, Jack P. Greene, Deborah E. Harkness, Mary Lindemann, Lary May, Thomas S. Mullaney, Jana Bouck Remy, Vanessa R. Schwartz, James J. Sheehan,** and **Jeffrey N. Wasserstrom**

EDITOR: Elise Lipkowitz
with assistance from Elisabeth Grant, Pillarisetti Sudhir, Liz Townsend, and Robert B. Townsend.

LAYOUT: Chris Hale
Cover photograph, *Route 50 near Lake Tahoe at Night*, is by Thomas Stanger.

© 2009 by the American Historical Association
ISBN: 978-0-87229-162-1

Library of Congress Cataloging-in-Publication data:

From concept to completion : a dissertation-writing guide for history students / by the AHA Graduate and Early Career Committee.

p. cm.

Includes bibliographical references.

ISBN 978-0-87229-162-1 (alk. paper)

1. History—Research—Handbooks, manuals, etc. 2. Academic writing—Handbooks, manuals, etc. 3. Dissertations, Academic—Handbooks, manuals, etc. I. American Historical Association. Graduate and Early Career Committee.

D16.F93 2008

808'.0669—dc22   2008028781

TABLE OF CONTENTS

PREFACE

You have finished your coursework. You have served as a teaching assistant for undergraduate courses. You have passed your qualifying exams. Ahead remains one final hurdle before you earn your PhD—a dissertation.

This pamphlet is designed to assist you in undertaking this important and, all too often, unnecessarily opaque and daunting task. While you will devise your research questions, pursue your research, and draw conclusions from your evidence, you should not need to wonder how to research and write a history dissertation. That is where this pamphlet comes in.

Filled with helpful tips, sage advice, and practical steps, *From Concept to Completion: A Dissertation-Writing Guide for History Students* makes transparent the process of formulating, researching, and writing a history dissertation. Twelve outstanding historians—Leora Auslander, Fitzhugh Brundage, Anthony Grafton, Jack Greene, Deborah Harkness, Mary Lindemann, Lary May, Thomas Mullaney, Jana Remy, Vanessa Schwartz, James Sheehan, and Jeffrey Wasserstrom—have graciously shared their wisdom about the various phases of this process from conceptualizing a project to the dissertation defense. This pamphlet is designed to be read cover to cover and also to be a resource to which you frequently return as you move from one phase of your dissertation to another.

This pamphlet would not have come to fruition without the assistance of many behind-the-scenes contributors. Sterling Fluharty, a PhD candidate at the University of Oklahoma, inspired the AHA's Graduate and Early Career Committee to undertake this project with a post on his blog—PhD in History—highlighting the need for such a publication. AHA Executive Director Arnita Jones and members of the AHA's Research and Professional Divisions and the AHA Council provided early and consistent support. The 2007 and 2008 AHA Graduate and Early Career Committee—Daniela Blei, Megan Feeney, Katherine Hijar, Ryan Linkoff, and Silvia Marsans-Sakly—worked tirelessly to recruit authors and to co-write the entry on the student's perspective on managing one's dissertation committee. Last but not least, AHA Assistant Directors Noralee Frankel and Robert B. Townsend proved indispensable to this pamphlet's conceptualization and editing while the AHA's Publications Production Manager Chris Hale has created a visually appealing pamphlet.

Elise Lipkowitz, Editor
Chair, AHA Graduate and Early Career Committee, 2006–present
Doctoral Candidate, Department of History, Northwestern University

1

Defining a History Dissertation and Its Role in One's Future Scholarship

By Jack P. Greene

If you aspire to contribute to historical knowledge—and if you have been
admitted to a doctoral program in history, there is every reason to suppose
that you do—your dissertation will be the most important component
of your graduate program. While the lecture courses you take are designed
to prepare you as a teacher, and the seminars are intended to develop your
critical thinking and research skills, the dissertation is meant to make you a
historian, a contributor to original knowledge in your field. Your dissertation
will have a profound effect upon your professional career. Its quality and
significance will provide a strong indication of whether or not you have the
makings of a historical analyst, one who combines imagination, research,
analytical skills, and mastery over a chosen field to produce significant works
of historical scholarship. Your dissertation will influence, if not determine,
the kind of position you ultimately obtain. Next to choosing a specific field
of study, selecting a dissertation subject is, far and away, the most important
choice you will have to make in your doctoral program. In making it, you will
confront three basic questions: (1) When should I choose a subject? (2) How
should I choose a subject? and (3) What kind of subject should I choose?

When Should I Choose a Subject?

The answer to this question is, as soon as possible. The dissertation will require
a major investment of your energies for several years, and those who wait to
choose and define a topic until they have passed their field examinations are
likely to add a year or more to the process. To avoid needlessly extending

your doctoral program—not to mention accumulating more debt—it is highly desirable, some would say imperative, to begin casting for a topic right away, at the very beginning of your doctoral program. A few people enter graduate school with the benefit of an undergraduate thesis introducing them to a subject that they like and can see developing into a doctoral dissertation. If that is not the case with you, you should approach every course or seminar with a view, first, to choosing a major field of concentration and, second, finding a dissertation topic that will make a contribution to that field. Reading insightfully for your courses can sometimes lead you into a promising and congenial subject, while writing a seminar paper on it can familiarize you with the sources you will need to consult, provide you with an opportunity to explore the subject's parameters and implications, and enable you and your advisors to assess whether it has the potential to lead to an important piece of historical scholarship. It is all too easy to get bogged down in reading for courses and examinations during the years when you are preparing for your field examinations, but the wise student will also take time to consider how, after passing those examinations, she or he can hit the ground running, ready to jump into intensive research.

Choosing a dissertation subject early will yield other benefits. It enables you to shape your program of courses and seminars to get the widest possible perspective on your subject and develop it to the fullest. It gives you time to find a new topic if the first one turns out to be hard to define, difficult to research, or simply uncongenial. It provides you with an intellectual focus that will help keep you from losing sight of your long-term goals as you pursue success in course and field examinations, success that, however essential, will not turn out to be nearly as important to your development as a historian as producing a solid and thoughtful dissertation.

How Should I Choose a Subject?

Some advisors assign dissertation subjects, and occasionally such an assigned topic works out satisfactorily. However, it is far better in such an important undertaking for *you* to choose the topic and work out its dimensions yourself. Historians who succeed in producing work that makes an impact on their fields invariably exhibit a high degree of independent-mindedness, and the goal of doctoral study should be to produce independent-minded analysts, who, with a little advice, can work out their own topics and diagnose the larger questions that a topic might illuminate. A good advisor will always steer students away from a topic that is too demanding for a first research project, or calls for skills that they do not possess, or is unlikely to yield a strong dissertation. But an advisor should also grant students their impulses in the choice of a subject that will consume several years of their lives. Choosing and defining a dissertation topic can be an important early step in helping you to achieve your intellectual independence and develop the confidence of a scholar who has contributed to her or his chosen field of study. You—not your advisor—have to live with this topic and nurse it to fruition, and only you can predict whether a given subject will sustain your interest during the long process of defining, researching, and writing a substantial work. All too many people pass their field examinations but never finish their dissertations, because they simply lose interest in them. Your topic should not be merely congenial. Ideally, you should fall madly in love with it and pursue it with the passion and dedication of a lover.

Practical considerations also enter into choosing a dissertation topic. If you do not already possess the necessary intellectual, linguistic, and technical skills, you need to consider the cost of acquiring them in terms of time and money. Also, the topic needs to be researchable. Rarely are history students able to find all the sources they need in their own university libraries. When picking a topic you need to consider where the sources are and how you will manage to get to them for the extended period, usually no less than a year, that will be required. What resources are available from your university, the government or foundations, or research libraries to support a year of research? To produce a work that is both substantial and persuasive you will need to build a solid research base and to exploit it as fully as possible.

What Kind of Subject Should I Choose?

Many students choose their dissertation topic simply because it fills a gap in historical knowledge. Some scholars even succeed in publishing their revised dissertations for no better reason than that. However, works of this limited aspiration and character often serve as important building blocks for others. Whether a subject has had a lot of attention or none should not be your prime consideration. Eschewing intellectual timidity, you should evaluate every topic you consider in terms of its potential to change the landscape of your field and should keep this goal in mind as you move through the construction of your dissertation. Whether by showing the crucial relevance of a neglected topic or by putting a more familiar topic in a new light, your object is to compel scholars in your field to re-evaluate the way they have traditionally understood it.

To meet this engaging and demanding objective is never easy, but the good news is that it is engaging precisely because it is demanding. A how-to manual might break the process of dissertation writing into the four stages of definition, research, analysis, and writing. Each of these stages generates it own gratifications: the excitement of finding and defining a congenial and important topic, the thrill of discovery as you conduct your research, the challenge of analyzing and organizing your data, and the satisfaction of drawing it all together into a coherent and well-organized whole. But these stages are ideally intertwined and overlapping. As you get deeper and deeper into your research, you will discover that the topic itself changes shape, presenting unanticipated questions and possibilities, even raising doubts about the very assumptions with which you began; and this engaging process is likely to continue and intensify as you move on to the interrogation and analysis of your research materials and to the organization and writing of chapters. At every stage, you will be wrestling with the elusive goals of wringing every last drop of interpretational meaning out of your materials, marshaling your data to formulate a significant problem, and developing a general argument that speaks to, refines, or even transforms the larger issues in your field. As you do so, you may find yourself redefining what you intend to do. Ultimately, it is your responsibility to explain fully and explicitly to your readers what you have done and why it is important. To leave it to reviewers to discover and point out the larger meaning of your work means that you have left the most vital part of the enterprise to others, and this may be as deeply embarrassing as having your work judged as poorly researched, weakly analyzed, or carelessly organized, written, and argued.

The complexity of this process suggests the need to cultivate a high level of intellectual flexibility, but while writing your dissertation you will also need to develop a second intellectual quality that goes into the making of a successful historian. A healthy dose of skepticism always serves the historian well. A wariness of received wisdom, a suspicion of existing orthodoxies, a critical stance toward current interpretational fashions—all can lead you to find new and more convincing ways of utilizing the documentation in your field and expanding the intellectual parameters of scholarship in it, while a measure of critical awareness about your own predispositions concerning human behavior may help you to transcend some of your own blind spots and to see things in your data that you might otherwise have missed.

Finally, it always helps to get a critical response to your dissertation at every stage of its construction. Advisors are a prime source for such a response, as are conferences and professional meetings, where you can try out your ideas on specialists in your area. But some of the best advice and most exciting interactions come from peers with their own independent interests in your field or adjacent ones. If your department does not have a formal seminar at which doctoral students can present their work for criticism and suggestions—and many departments do not—then you should take the lead and organize an informal one. You will never regret it.

The dissertation may be the most demanding and onerous requirement for the PhD in history, but it is also the most important, the most exciting, and the most engaging. None of the other requirements provides you with so much opportunity to develop the research, analytic, and writing skills you will need to become a productive and recognized scholar. Those who learn those essential skills and go on to identify and try to resolve other historical problems may well find that the continuing quest to understand the past will engage them for the rest of their lives.

2

THE GENESIS OF A DISSERTATION: FROM CHOOSING A TOPIC TO DEVELOPING A DISSERTATION PROPOSAL

By **Leora Auslander**

Let me start with the obvious. The central criterion in choosing a dissertation topic is that it be one that interests you. It is also important that it be a good fit with your intellectual strengths and your life circumstances. Ideally, you will be living with your topic for a long time—from its genesis as a proposal through its ultimate publication as a book. In less happy outcomes, the topic becomes a hindrance to finishing your degree or to getting that first book completed. It turns out, in fact, that the seemingly obvious task of choosing a dissertation topic isn't always all that obvious, and much can get in the way of finding an appropriate one.

Some graduate students are lucky; they have a burning question to which they *must* know the answer. That question is, furthermore, accessible to the tools of the discipline, sources exist and are available, the student already has the skills needed to effectively research it, the question is one that immediately strikes other historians as significant, and it is a project a faculty member in the student's department is well equipped to advise. This ideal conjunction is rare. More often history graduate students find themselves, as they approach the end of coursework or complete their preliminary exams, intrigued by many questions and by many historical methodologies. They may have a topic, but no sources; a fascinating archive, but no driving question; both a problem and documentation, but be lacking a vital skill. Many students also get side tracked by anxiety, convinced that if only they can identify the next "hot" topic, their professional future will be assured. The "right" topic will produce research and grants, postdoctoral fellowships, and ultimately a tenure-track job.

Unless you are one of the very few for whom all has simply come together, the first step is to think very honestly about the historical *questions* that engage you and the *historiography* you find most compelling. An effective strategy here is simply to make a list of the books you have read that when you put them down you sighed and thought, "I wish I had written that!" Or, if there was a book or a course that made you decide to pursue graduate work in history, re-read it or go back over your notes. Then reflect on what it is, precisely, that you found so compelling. Was it the questions asked? The rhetorical style? The evidence used? This contemplation should narrow the field of possible subdisciplines. If the books that most fascinate you all attempt to explain mass social or political movements, then that's an indication of the kind of project you should pursue. If, by contrast, they all explicate a cultural or intellectual current, object, or individual's oeuvre, then that's a signpost towards a different route. If they tend to be micro-histories of a small town or a family, or macro-histories of nation-states, that too is significant. At this point you should be able to think of a few possible open puzzles or debates within your historical expertise that are amenable to the kind of history you want to write.

The second step is to evaluate the kind of historical *research* for which you have the necessary skills and that you enjoy doing. Some kinds of projects will have you largely sitting in libraries reading perfectly legible printed books. Some will have you in archives opening mysterious carton after mysterious carton, spending minutes if not hours simply figuring out what the stuff is before trying to read it. Actually reading it may pose its own challenges of handwriting, language use, and fragmentation. Many projects fall in between, requiring some library and some archival work. Other dissertations force you to "make" your own archive—you have to persuade individuals, families, organizations, or businesses to let you look at their private documents. Some require taking seemingly trivial, ephemeral materials—telephone books, restaurant menus, knitting patterns—and constructing a narrative out of them. Some provide an opportunity for you to talk with people and to do oral histories. Some require skills in other disciplines—art or architectural history, statistics, cartography, musicology, or archaeology. Some will demand that you learn languages you don't yet know. Some will require several years of residence abroad; some will keep you moving from one town to another, following an archival trail; some can be done from your university library. It is essential to look at your own intellectual and craft-skill strengths and weaknesses honestly. Some limitations or gaps can be effectively addressed, but some should be lived with, and a topic chosen that accommodates them.

In addition to one's intellectual talents, skills, and tastes, one's life circumstances also matter. Being attached or single; without kids or with; gay, straight, transsexual, or bi; Asian American, black, Latino, or white; religiously observant or not—all shape what is actually practicable and what is not. Seek advice on these questions, and not only from your official advisor. Not all faculty or fellow students know what it's like to live a particular place as a woman, or what childcare facilities are likely to exist, or how comfortable it is to be black or lesbian. Those are all legitimate and necessary considerations in the choice of a dissertation topic.

Unfortunately, the question of what kind of history one wants to write, and what kind of history one is best suited or able to write, are not the same. A few examples may clarify this point. One may very much enjoy reading social histories, books that grapple with how life was lived, experienced, and interpreted by marginally literate or illiterate people, but not in fact have the great patience or good imagination to find possible sources, tolerance for reading texts that are not intrinsically interesting, willingness to spend a long time in the field, and the required auxiliary skills in other disciplines. One may find quantitative analyses of production and consumption fascinating, but have no talent for the statistics and the construction of databases essential to this approach. One may be unable to put down intellectual histories that parse and explain a corpus of complex philosophical arguments, but lack the skill to read texts closely and analyze the cultural milieu of the texts.

After you have made your initial lists—of the books you would have liked to have written; of the historical questions that move you; of your intellectual tastes and proclivities; of the possibilities and constraints of your life circumstances—you should be ready to write up a final, short list of possible topics. At this point, in addition to brainstorming with colleagues and teachers, you should turn your attention seriously to the existing historiography and source possibilities. What has been written on, or related to, this topic? If it's an area in which no one seems to have written for a long time, why is that? If a great deal has been produced in the last ten years, is there really room for you? What kinds of sources might there be? Where are they? What new skills do you need to learn? Do you really want to do so? Do not try to decide what the marketable topic in four years will be; we are historians, not fortune tellers. From your short list, again ideally in consultation, make a decision.

If there is any question of the fit between the topic one wants to take up and its feasibility (both in general and for you in particular), it is extremely helpful to find a grant that enables you do a couple of months of pre-dissertation research. These short research trips will allow you to discover *before* you are completely committed to a topic whether or not it's a good topic—in all of the senses discussed above—for you. The work they enable will also facilitate writing effective dissertation proposals and grant applications.

By the time you are at the point of applying for pre-dissertation grants, however, you will have had to choose your dissertation advisor and perhaps your committee. Both of these choices may be very obvious; there may be only one faculty member whose field specialization makes it appropriate for her or him to chair your committee and the same may be true of the other members of the committee. Often, however, there is a choice, in which case some useful questions to ask are: Is the professor someone with whom you find it helpful and easy to brainstorm? Have you found the feedback on earlier work with that faculty member helpful? Is her or his intellectual and professional approach one you find compatible? Your relationship with your thesis advisor will, hopefully, continue for many years. S/he will see you through graduate school, into your first (and sometimes subsequent) jobs, provide advice about publishing your first book, and write recommendations for you for a very long time. You should not, therefore, choose a thesis advisor on the basis of who is on leave, or not, in a given year. Second, third, and fourth readers should be selected together to compose a complementary dissertation committee. They are often chosen to provide thematic or methodological expertise. Or they may be faculty with whom you have a good brainstorming relationship, or whom you find to be particularly good readers. There is no one model for a successful relationship between students and their dissertation committees, but good communication and shared expectations obviously help a great deal.

Once you have assembled your dissertation committee, most history departments require some form of proposal. The proposal has several purposes. First, it provides you with a map of your project for the next couple of years. It is very easy, even necessary, to lose sight of the big picture as you work your way through the sources. It is crucial, therefore, to have a clear statement of the larger goals—the main theme, the key questions, and the fields of study—to which you can refer after a few months of collecting archival dust. Needless to say, this picture changes over time as you work on your thesis. Second, the proposal allows your committee to provide the best possible assistance to you in moving the dissertation from a dream to a reality. Your committee can only be useful if it really understands the project. Finally, it is a text you can show other scholars over the next few years that will give them a clear sense of what you're doing. Dissertation proposals should be detailed enough to provide a clear map of the questions being asked and their significance, the relevant historiography, the conceptual framework, the sources as known, and your research strategy. On the other hand, it does not need to be a book in itself and should not attempt the impossible of stating the conclusions of research not yet done.

Dissertations are professional credentials. Much more significantly, however, researching and writing a dissertation is a magnificent adventure. The best dissertations, and the ones that earn people the best jobs, are not the ones that "fill a gap" nor the ones thought to be the next "hot topic," but rather the ones their authors were driven to write.

3

MANAGING YOUR
DISSERTATION COMMITTEE

By the AHA Graduate and Early Career Committee

Throughout the dissertation process, you should benefit from input—both from your committee and other scholars in the field. Maximizing the utility of your committee and other readers can make the journey more enjoyable and rewarding. Below are suggestions on how to navigate this process successfully and take ownership of your dissertation.

CHOOSE A COMMITTEE

Start early. Begin thinking about your committee's composition as early as possible. Early in your coursework years, take stock of your self, your interests, and your work style. Consider what skills, knowledge base, and support structure will assist you in completing a dissertation. Assess your expectations of an advising relationship: do you want a hands-off advisor who leaves space for your creativity or would you like someone to more closely monitor your progress?

DO YOUR HOMEWORK

Use coursework and especially individual reading courses to get to know various faculty members and their work styles. Consider potential advisors' accessibility, the timeliness and the quality of their feedback, their management style, their experience in mentoring PhDs, and the average time to degree for their advisees. Check professors' curriculum vitae and investigate their scholarly track record. Before you ask a faculty member to be on your committee, familiarize yourself with departmental/university guidelines regarding committee composition (for example, required number and desirability or feasibility of including advisors outside your institution). Then make an appointment with each professor you are considering to discuss your dissertation idea and gauge their level of interest in working with you. The greater their interest, the more likely they will be to sustain their engagement. Before formally asking them to be on your committee, talk with graduate students who work with them about each faculty member's strengths and weaknesses as a dissertation committee member.

THINK BALANCE

Your committee should provide four things: project guidance (such as aid with conceptualization, research design, and writing), geographic or time period expertise, advocacy, and encouragement. Given that it is nearly impossible to expect excellence in all four areas from any given person, choose committee members whose strengths complement one another. Make sure that you have someone who excels in at least one of these tasks. Remember to put a "cheerleader" on your committee. Select people who get along with each other; you do not want to be caught in the middle of a personal or professional dispute. Consider the benefits of an outside reader or arranging for someone in your field at another institution to give you feedback outside the traditional committee structure.

ASSIGN ROLES

The chair will work most closely with you. Choose someone within the same temporal and spatial field (for example, early modern France or colonial Latin America) but also consider his or her topical interests. Ask about the potential advisor's availability and leave schedule so you can plan accordingly. You want the chair to focus attention on your work; find out what s/he cares most deeply about and look for complementary research interests. You are investing in a long-term emotional and professional relationship. Select someone who can offer valuable insight, advocate for you, and suggest the next strategic move.

Secondary readers are typically less involved than your primary advisor. They may want to read more polished drafts, perhaps not until the penultimate stage. Do not ask secondary or tertiary readers to do the work of a chair, such as reading multiple drafts of grant applications or chapters or writing numerous recommendation letters.

Plan for the unexpected. Leave room in your committee so that you can alter its composition if your research or interests take you in another direction. Remember that by agreeing to serve on your committee, everyone, and especially your chair, is affirming that your research is worthwhile and that you are capable of high-quality work.

MANAGE YOUR COMMITTEE

Manage the advising relationship with clear, consistent, and effective communication. Keep your committee informed of your progress, even if it has been minimal. Ask for help when needed—being an independent learner does not mean working alone. If you fail to meet a deadline, do not hide; acknowledge that you are late, devise a new deadline, and keep working. Negotiate turn-around time for feedback. Ask each committee member what needs to be included in the dissertation for him or her to approve it, and keep a file of all correspondence.

BE PROFESSIONAL

Begin to see yourself as a professional in training, an intellectual apprentice who will soon join the cadre of future faculty, and act accordingly. When you meet with committee members, be prompt and have an agenda. If you cannot make your scheduled appointment, cancel ahead of time. When submitting work, prepare a cover sheet with an outline of your document indicating the kind of feedback you are looking for and how the chapter fits into your dissertation. Always bring a hard copy of the chapter to be discussed with you. Take notes at meetings so you will remember everything once you leave the office. Be courteous of professors' schedules. Give professors sufficient lead time for letters of recommendation and arrange mutually convenient times for meeting and submitting drafts.

Negative feedback is part of this process and is given in the spirit of improving your work. To minimize its impact, share your work with friends, classmates, or a dissertation writing group before showing it to faculty. In fact, participation in a writing group is often an invaluable source of "advising" and support for dissertators.

Ultimately, you need to decide on your argument and how your chapters will be structured. Demonstrating that you are in charge (with the power to respectfully disagree when warranted) will positively affect how your committee responds to you.

4

MANAGING THE COMMITTEE: A FACULTY MEMBER'S PERSPECTIVE

By W. Fitzhugh Brundage

Managing your dissertation committee may seem at times to require the patience of a saint and ample reserves of fortitude and tact. But just tell yourself that the experience is excellent preparation for the administrative chores and departmental politics that await you when you land a tenure-track job. And, like many things in graduate school, what once was vexing may grow more humorous over time as you recall your dissertation committee through the soft focus of nostalgia.

Communication is of paramount importance in your relationship with your committee. Keep committee members abreast of any developments they should know about. E-mail makes it easy for you to check in with your committee periodically and to inform them of your progress and any challenges or detours. By providing your committee with clear and concise summaries of your progress you'll ensure that you don't spring any surprises on them. Moreover, if you have alerted your committee members to important upcoming dates—such as committee meetings or deadlines for the submission of letters of recommendation—they are more likely to fulfill their obligations and do so in a timely manner. Requests for letters of recommendation submitted a week before the due date and last-minute announcements of early morning meetings are never greeted warmly.

It's also important to know when not to communicate with your committee. Although family and friends may welcome annual Christmas e-mails, photos of pets and vacation vistas, or links to blog entries, committee members probably won't. Communications with your committee should address professional issues and request specific and reasonable actions of the committee members. Let your committee know what you need, why you need it, and when you need it.

Good communication can also help you navigate any interpretative, ideological, and/or theoretical divisions among your committee. If you know that committee members are skeptical of your favored approach to your research question, it behooves you to provide them with ample opportunity to critique your work at every stage of the process. Don't shy away from sharing your work with such a committee member. It is far better to work through these differences informally than to wait until committee meetings or your dissertation defense to tangle with your methodological adversary. Moreover, a conscientious and responsible scholar who has received draft dissertation chapters in a timely fashion and has signed off on them cannot, in good conscience, subsequently challenge the completed dissertation. In the language of contemporary commercial speak, you want buy-in by your committee members and communication with them is the best way to achieve it.

Fortitude and tact are necessary when you deal with your committee members because they, like you, are overworked. How much you can ask of them will depend on your relationship with them and their obligations to you. You should have no qualms about asking your advisor for all manner of advice and letters of recommendation. But don't assume that the fifth member of your committee, who may be in a different department and know you solely on the basis of your dissertation prospectus or a single class, will be as forthcoming with letters or advice. Set reasonable expectations of your committee members.

With that in mind, be polite but persistent until you get what you need from your committee. Despite your care in selecting a committee you may find yourself with a committee member who is unwilling to properly fulfill professional obligations. In that case, discuss the matter with your advisor. If the advisor isn't sufficiently helpful, or in the unfortunate event that the advisor *is* the problem, seek out your director of graduate studies (DGS). A responsible DGS will handle awkward matters with discretion, so don't hesitate to discuss committee problems with him or her. If necessary, broach the matter with the department chair. Further afield, perhaps your graduate school has an ombudsman or an administrator who is charged with helping graduate students deal with difficult problems. Whatever the specific case on your campus, seek advice and support from appropriate administrators.

Managing the Committee: A Faculty Member's Perspective

Finally, the graduate secretary or administrative assistant in your department is likely to be an invaluable resource when questions arise about your committee. Departmental staff members tend to be storehouses of institutional memory and can offer advice on dealing with surly faculty, obstinate bureaucrats, punctilious administrators, and other challenges you may confront. Avail yourself of their knowledge and you will undoubtedly ease your path through your graduate program.

$$\boxed{5}$$

BOWLING FOR DOLLARS: THE ART OF WRITING THE GRANT PROPOSAL

By Vanessa R. Schwartz

Every PhD student in history, even those rare students fully funded through all years of study, should apply for research grants during the course of their graduate careers. Applying for funding constitutes an essential part of what faculty must do in order to support their research. Learning the art of grant writing in graduate school not only increases the chances that a student will complete the dissertation in a timely manner but provides training for a lifelong professional activity, as almost no form of support for research, including sabbatical support, comes without writing a proposal for the work to be conducted. In addition, external recognition of the value of your dissertation could make a diffence as you go on the job market.

Even the unsuccessful proposal advances the student's career because there is no better way to think about the significance of a proposed dissertation than by being forced to convince intelligent strangers about its importance in four to ten pages. And even if you do not succeed in obtaining a grant, your project is now known to senior faculty outside of your own institution. Some readers may be quite enamored of your project, and are disappointed when they rate you highly and you do not get the grant. They may well remember you in the future when jobs are available or publication opportunities arise. Thus, successful or not, every proposal matters and is a key way of joining the broader community of scholars and "going public" with your project. This is why grant writing is not to be taken lightly.

There are scholars who seem to have a way of thinking, as well as the sort of project, that lends itself to condensed explanation. Even if you are among the majority of scholars for whom that is not the case, you still have a chance of winning a grant. Before you begin, it is essential to understand that given the large numbers of applicants and the small numbers of funded proposals, no one has "a good chance" of winning. In addition, prizewinning first books did not always begin as winners of Social Science Research Council grants and Fulbright fellowships. Many brilliant historians were not successful in getting outside funding for their dissertation research. Sometimes that can be due to the tastes of the selection committee, the fashions of the times, or the fact that some projects are more interesting as finished products than as proposals. Sometimes it is because a student had a great project but wrote a weak proposal. This essay is meant to help you write a strong proposal.

BEFORE THE PROPOSAL WRITING BEGINS

Find a Compelling Project

Behind every successful proposal is an excellent research question and problem. This means that before you write a proposal, you must identify a problem that goes beyond gap-filling and the logic of "no one has ever studied this here and in this time." All proposals should try to answer the following questions: What will we learn that we do not already know? Why should we care? How will we know that the research results are valid? Otherwise put, a successful proposal must begin with a dissertation topic/problem that answers the most basic question: so what?

In order to answer that question, you need to take several steps.

1. Master the secondary literature narrowly attached to your field of specialization as well as the "big books" that will enable you to frame your questions beyond your time/place designations.

2. Select a research method to answer the questions you pose. This will address what you might think of as the "how" question. In order to select your method(s) you need to have engaged questions of theory and method. Sometimes the research itself will demand a shift in methods and assumptions, which is why knowing theory and methodology will be helpful in the short term and the long run.

3. Clarify in your own mind what "interdisciplinary" means if you are claiming this as an aspect of your dissertation. Do not "assert" interdisciplinarity. Think about why it is a value added to historical research.

4. Identify a corpus of research materials related to the problem at hand.

Identify Possible Funding Sources

Funding sources are ever-evolving. On the one hand, there are the "big grants" in the field that your advisor and their previous students know about and/or have received. These should not take much time to identify. There are, however, grants associated with library collections and archives that are also excellent sources of smaller funds.

Identify deadlines and give yourself and those on whom you are relying for letters of support plenty of time. The first time you write a series of grant proposals for a project, expect that it will go through several rounds of revisions. You should work on this with your letter writers (who anyway need to read the proposal in advance) and possibly with other students and faculty at your university. Seek out grant writing workshops or ask for them to be held. It will help to have the proposal vetted by intelligent strangers since that is who your screeners and selection committee will be.

Write the Proposal Itself

Follow some general guidelines when you are writing the actual proposal.

1. Establish the context for your work. Not everyone is an expert on what you are studying or understands why they should care. Think about how you can get your reader "up to speed" with a body of knowledge in only two or three paragraphs at most.

2. Consider the "context" as a series of nesting dolls. Move from the specificity of the problem you are addressing to the largest questions and issues that can be better understood by virtue of the work you are undertaking.

3. Aim for absolute clarity of language. Proposals are read not only by historians outside your area of specialization but also by humanists and social scientists from other disciplines. Avoid pretentious jargon and neologisms of any kind.

Instead, be a tour guide through the field's research frontiers. Convey your unabashed enthusiasm for your problem and materials and remember the proposal is a "pitch" of sorts.

4. Carefully follow whatever protocols for the proposal the funding agency outlines. This can lead to writing ten different proposals for ten agencies. The key is to be aware of the call for proposals and follow it. Understand that there are ways to frame your project that might be more compatible with an agency's goals or requirements. Be careful to communicate any special aspects to your letter writers who can also tailor their letters to the requirements of the granting agency.

5. Describe the feasibility of the research in terms of method, materials, and time. You need to make a case that you know how to answer your research questions, that there are sufficient research materials available and accessible to you as a researcher, and that you are proposing a reasonable work plan for the duration of the grant and for the scope of a dissertation.

There are also several specific aspects of the proposal you should consider.

1. Choose the title wisely and with two things in mind: to signal the subject and parameters of the project and suggest a perspective or point of view.

2. Much is gained or lost in the first few sentences of a proposal. Screeners are reviewing many proposals and they are tired and agitated by how much material they have to read. Your first sentence should be about your subject or have a great anecdote about the past. It should not be about the scholarship. Historians are overrepresented in humanities fellowship competitions partly because they tell good stories. Be as fresh, original, and interesting as your material no doubt is.

3. You should have a strong working hypothesis and/or research question that can be expressed in one sentence. This should come not long after the attention-grabbing opening. People often think of this as the essential phrase of the "elevator" version of your dissertation (that is, a description that lasts as long as an elevator ride).

4. Avoid use of the first person. While you will certainly need to do this when you describe your research plan, otherwise speak of the project rather than yourself.

5. Justify the reasons for your research positively. If you say you are filling a gap, you are advancing through negation. What is "missing" may well be missing for good reason and what has been considered endlessly may well deserve further inquiry and explanation.

6. Make good use of telling detail and illustration. Your reader needs examples and details from the "stuff" of your research. Even if you haven't conducted months of research, by the time you are ready to write your grant proposal you will have gathered some interesting details that animate your thought. Engage your reader with great "stuff."

7. As you conclude your proposal, return to what is at stake in the project. Remember, these are the big questions that transcend time, place, and sometimes disciplinary specificity.

Whether you are successful or not in any given request for funding, you should see each proposal as a "version" of a project that is constantly in development. Each time you submit a new proposal, you need to plan for it and re-write the old proposal. If you have been unsuccessful in a fellowship competition, ask the granting agency for feedback as some even provide screener comments and evaluation. You will never really know why you did not get a grant. It is, however, in your best interest and within your power to constantly work to make the proposal the strongest it can be. The rest is bowling for dollars.

6

ORGANIZING MATERIALS FROM ARCHIVES TO DISSERTATION

By Anthony Grafton

The notes you take while researching a dissertation can and should become some of your most treasured possessions: a rich and reliable quarry from which you can draw the components for your dissertation, and which will serve you for years thereafter. But to build a scholarly apparatus of high quality, you must work systematically and accurately from the very start of your research: in fact, from the time when you begin work on your proposal. As C. Wright Mills showed long ago, building a proper system for keeping files and bringing it up to date regularly is a central task for anyone engaged in systematic enquiry.

These directions may seem quaint: forty years ago, graduate students groaned through first-year methods courses that concentrated not on theory but on the choice of file-card formats for note taking. But they mattered then, and they matter now. More than one intelligent and productive scholar has been forced out of the historical profession, and many have seen their careers damaged by negative reviews and assessments, because they offered readers and critics sloppy, second-hand, or simply incorrect documentation. The more controversial the subject you are studying, the more likely that other scholars will examine what you write with a hostile eye. More important, it's simply your duty, whatever your subject, to make your dissertation and the articles and book that you base on it as accurate as you can. To be a good scholar, you must start by becoming a good artisan.

First things first: trust no one. Never rely on a quotation in a secondary work, however brilliant and learned the author; always check the original. Never rely on existing bibliographical aids, either. Even the most elaborate catalogues of manuscripts and archives have mistakes in attribution, dating, and pagination. These can carry over into your work if you don't verify everything in the original. Computerized library catalogues are as dangerous as they are indispensable. Titles in foreign languages and older, complex titles in English often swarm with misprints, even in the catalogues of the British Library and other national collections. Examine everything yourself, with your own eyes. Above all, never believe anyone who tells you that a source has been used exhaustively.

Once you have adopted the proper, skeptical attitude, you can choose a bibliographical format and develop a single bibliography. From the start you should record bibliographical data and locations for all archival, manuscript, and printed sources that you consult, primary or secondary. Use a consistent form and keep a single, running bibliography. By doing so, you will free yourself to use a consistent system of abbreviation (for example, author and short-title or author and date) in all of your own notes and in all your citations. You will save yourself worries later on, when you may have to revise your work in a hurry, far from the Asian, Latin American, or European collections where you did your research. You will also make it easy for your reader to follow in your footsteps, which is the whole point of citation.

Virtually all PhD candidates keep their notes in electronic form, and those who do must choose the software with which to keep records. Many history graduate students find that EndNote works very well: you can use it to carry out searches, to build up both a bibliography and a library of texts in electronic form, and to create citations in the format proper to your subject. You can also import bibliographical references directly—but see above, under skepticism, and remember that doing this without checking can be hazardous to the health of your scholarship.

Whether you use EndNote or one of its rivals, it normally makes sense to keep your notes in the same program and in the same series of files in which you keep your bibliographical references. More important than the form of electronic storage that you choose, however, is the quality of attention that you bring to the process of collecting, sorting, and assessing materials. For it is as you fashion the raw materials from the archive into the beams, planks, and panels in your own collection that you determine the foundations of the structures to come—or undermine everything that you will later do.

In taking notes, you are creating a personal archive. Its components will take many different forms: transcripts from archival documents, manuscripts, and rare books; digital photographs of those and other sources; microfilms or scans; downloaded books, articles, and documents in PDF or other formats; video or audio materials. Whatever the nature of your materials, several systematic principles should guide you as you store them and put them into order.

Security comes first. In the 1970s, we kept our boxes of file cards and piles of manuscript in the refrigerator, in the hope of preserving them from fire. Nowadays, you should have duplicate sets of your electronic files in multiple forms of storage. Never trust your files to the vulnerable hard drive of the laptop that you carry around with you. At the very least, store copies of all your files on memory sticks (but bear in mind that these are easy to lose) or send them to your own e-mail account (Gmail offers a great deal of space for free, secure backup). Ideally, though, your files should be lodged and used on a computer all of whose files are backed up every day on a central server, in addition to an external hard drive or space on the web.

Second comes precision—precision in both storage and use of your sources. And precision means transforming raw information into usable notes. However you store your materials, be sure that every single item has a clear, unique file name, and that every file states its source. However many photographs or scans of documents you may have, be sure that you transcribe them—just as you would transcribe documents in an archive or library that did not permit photography—word for word before you set out to interpret them in your writing. By transcribing documents, you master their contents, you solve problems of decipherment and interpretation, and you produce a searchable text. Doing this makes the sources far more accessible to you—but the process has its risks. Most likely you will use a keyboard to do this job. Trust your fingers no farther than you trust catalogues. Once you have finished a transcript, check it—ideally by printing it out and comparing it with the original—and correct the inevitable slips.

Third comes tacit knowledge, which you should try to make explicit and to preserve. While you are working in an archives or a library, you will master its principles of organization and grasp the nature of particular collections. You will learn to read difficult scripts, come to recognize actors' handwriting, and gain broad knowledge of the forms of contemporary documents. And, if all goes as it should, you will exchange information on all these points with colleagues, librarians, and archivists. Record this information as you learn it, as you record the documents themselves. Otherwise you will find yourself writing your dissertation from decontextualized records, which you can no longer manage as skillfully as you could two or three years before, while you were actually working in the archives.

The last, but not the least important, stage in making your archive is the paper record. Some scholars—including some younger ones—continue to find that they prefer making notes on paper in the first instance. Most humans—even those who handle electronic databases most deftly—read texts on paper more perceptively and accurately than they can read texts on screen. Contemporary dissertation writers will certainly want to have direct electronic access to all notes—even those not originally recorded electronically. But in the end, a historian does not only cite documents, but interprets them, and the best way to do this is from a legible, accurate text on paper.

Ideally, then, once you have created your electronic archive, you will also print out at least those segments of it that you have created yourself. Arrange these files as carefully and systematically as you arrange their electronic counterparts, in the drawers of a file cabinet or in looseleaf notebooks. As soon as you start using them, you will find that they complement your electronic files, and that you know your materials far better by using both sets of files at once than you could ever know them from working entirely on screen.

Finally, you must decant all of this material—or at least all of it that is relevant—into your dissertation. When quoting a primary source in another language, you should translate it into idiomatic English in your text and quote the original, in full, in a footnote. If you merely refer to the source, then you need only quote the original in your note. In some cases, a reference to the file or volume in question will suffice. One simple principle can guide you: be sure that the next person interested in the field can use your work to gain a clear impression of the subject matter and the various kinds of sources. Once again, trust no one, including yourself: check every quotation and reference against the original or your closest facsimile of it—which should, of course, be readily available in your lucidly organized personal archive.

7

DELVING INTO THE DISSERTATION

By Jeffrey N. Wasserstrom

One tough thing about writing a dissertation, after having done the research, is creating a picture in your mind's eye of what the finished product will look like. And this is important, especially if you are one of those (like me) who think that it makes sense to treat the dissertation as a book-in-the-making. Some people will tell you that a thesis is a thesis, not the first draft of a monograph. But whether or not you ultimately decide you need to make radical changes to the manuscript before sending it to a publisher, it seems to me to make good practical sense to strive to create something that at least has the potential to be transformed into a book without being totally revised. As a result, having an overall vision of where you are headed when you start writing is invaluable.

One thing you will have going for you is that to get funding to do your research, or at some schools simply to be advanced to candidacy, you will have already had to write up plans of action. So I will focus here partly on the value but also the limitations later on of those early getting-ready-to-go-into-the-field exercises.

When you return from the archives, one helpful thing to do is simply take a fresh look what you wrote before you headed off. If nothing else, it may be amusing to see just how far you've diverged from your original plans. There's also a chance that re-reading those early exercises will give you a sense that you already have a workable skeleton onto which you can simply start putting some flesh.

This is not always as easy as it might seem, however, for two reasons. First, plans can—and often should—change due to what the archives contain. You might well find, for example, as I did, that there were so few documents relevant to what was supposed to be a major part of your study and so many rich materials about what was supposed to be a minor one that you will deal with the former in only a few pages and devote whole chapters to the latter.

Second, in a grant proposal or a dissertation prospectus, it is easy to fudge things. Grant agencies don't typically require a chapter-by-chapter breakdown of the thesis, for example, nor do they ask for details about how you will organize the material you gather and begin to put words on the page. A prospectus may or may not need to describe how much of a thesis will be devoted to a particular topic. The readers of these materials are just interested in getting a sense of the issues you'll address, the materials you'll rely upon, and the contribution your dissertation will make to one or more fields. When you have done your research, the chance to fudge is gone. The words have to get onto the page somehow; you need to have a sense of what the chapters will be.

Still, some of the same things that I found helpful in drafting dissertation grant proposals (at Berkeley in the 1980s, I didn't have to write a prospectus) also ended up seeming useful when it came time to sit down to write—and these things have continued to prove beneficial when taking on subsequent projects. Here, then, are some of the things that I found it useful to do when I was applying for funding to go to China to explore the history of Shanghai protests of the Republican period (1912–49)—and some of the ways I modified them when I started to write.

One thing I did then was to spend some time reflecting on books I'd read recently and admired. I then tried to figure out why I thought they worked so well. Next, I asked myself if any of them seemed to have the potential to serve as a model for my project.

As a China specialist, I see this as reflecting my Confucian side, since Confucius was a big proponent of model emulation. One became good, in his mind, by finding people to admire and trying to be like them, as well as reading up on the ancient sages and trying to follow in their footsteps.

Something worth stressing is that, when looking for models, it is important that the fit not be too perfect. In other words, it will create problems if you seize on a work that is too close to what you want to undertake. There need to be areas of difference as well as things that resonate between what someone else has done and what you are setting out to do. I also find it crucial when looking for models—and here I part company from Confucius, who was a big fan of awe-inspiring sages—to latch onto works that impress me but don't completely blow me away. I need to be able to see some flaws and limitations. Picking a model that is too close to home or too awe-inspiring can be dangerous, since this can stifle creativity, leading one to create something that's just a slight variation an extant work, or prove paralyzing, as you begin to worry that your own creation cannot possibly live up to the Platonic ideal that a beloved book represents.

In my own case, I began my research proposal reflections by thinking about E. P. Thompson's *The Making of the English Working Class*, which I had read as an undergraduate and then again in graduate school. Like so many other historians of my generation (and several other generations), I was awe-struck, finding the writing powerful, the research impressive, and the passion behind the arguments compelling. I almost immediately discarded it as a "model," though, despite (really, partly because of) all it had going for it. This was true despite the fact that it met the criteria of being similar in some ways yet different in others from what I was moving toward as a topic: I wanted to look at protests, a major focus in the book, but those of China rather than England. But I just knew, instinctively, that it would be a dangerous book to try to emulate—and not only because of the length (864 pages!).

I soon realized that there were a couple of other books that I had read that had better potential as models. These were both by George Rudé, like Thompson a leading light in the rise of the "new social history" in the 1960s. One was *The Crowd in History*, the other *The Crowd in the French Revolution*. I wasn't in awe of these books (or their author) in the same way that I was of Thompson and his masterpiece. I admired Rudé but didn't feel that he'd necessarily given us the last word on his subjects or created perfect or near perfect texts. And, of course, his subject was not exactly mine, since *The Crowd in History* dealt with two countries, neither of which was China, while *The Crowd in the French Revolution* dealt with a few years, not several decades.

Having selected my models, I took a mix and match approach, drawing on aspects of each of the books while crafting a grant proposal that had a singularly unimaginative name: "The Shanghai Crowd in the Chinese Revolution, 1911–49." Like *The Crowd in the French Revolution*, it stuck to one place. Like *The Crowd in History*, though, I envisioned my dissertation as eschewing a straightforward chronological framework, but rather containing different chapters devoted to specific kinds of popular actions, from Luddism (Shanghai rickshaw pullers had smashed streetcars) to strikes (Shanghai cotton mill workers launched many of those) to food riots (rice substituting in the Chinese case for bread in the European ones). I didn't provide a chapter-by-chapter outline in the grant proposals, but Rudé's two books, between them, certainly helped give me a sense of what the finished product might look like.

Not long after I got to China, I realized that it would be disastrous to stay wedded to the Rudé-based formula I had concocted. Why? Because the detailed police and magistrate reports that he (and Thompson) relied upon to analyze the social composition and modes of action taken by crowds of bread rioters just did not have Shanghai counterparts. The various local police forces in that partially colonized city compiled detailed reports about many things (especially underground Communist cells), but not about rice riots. All that they told me, which was not very helpful, was that on such and such a date, large groups stormed into such and such a rice shop.

There were other dead ends relating to sources, the most disappointing having to do with machine-breakers. I was fascinated by Luddism, which had not only attracted Rudé and Thompson's attention, but also that of Eric Hobsbawm, a third new social history hero of mine. How discouraging, then, to realize that the couple of mentions of rampaging rickshaw pullers I had come across in newspapers before heading to China were, in essence, all there was to work with, leaving little opportunity to test Hobsbawm's claims about Luddism being a form of "collective bargaining by riot," let alone finding counterparts to the rich folklore surrounding Captain Ludd analyzed so evocatively by Thompson.

On the other hand, some archival veins turned out to be richer than I had expected. The richest lodes of all related to labor strikes and student-led mass movements, each of which I had imagined would be the focus of but a chapter apiece. I learned that Shanghai labor strikes were the focus of a work-in-progress by another scholar, Elizabeth Perry (whose previous studies of rural unrest I thought superb), so it seemed logical for me to concentrate on campus unrest. An additional attraction was that there was already an excellent Shanghai-focused book on worker activism (by Emily Honig) that made use of approaches associated with the new social history (concern with daily life, for example), while previous analyses of Chinese students had tended to hew more closely to intellectual history and political history modes of analysis.

Returning to the analogy of Chinese philosophical schools, this was a case of abandoning my modified version of Confucianism and embracing my inner Daoist (Taoist)—since a core belief of Daoism is the value of going with the flow. Being able to adjust to what comes your way rather than stick to a predetermined course of action, just as the water in a river moves around obstacles in its path, is prized by Lao Zi (Lao Tzu).

In the end, though, a Confucian interest in order needed to come back into play. So, when I returned from the field with an enormous amount of material on a subject that was originally supposed to comprise just a single chapter, I began trying to cast around for new models. I went back to works I had read in the past (studies of collective action by Charles Tilly and Natalie Davis and books on Chinese student movements, among them) that now took on new relevance, due to my increased interest in a particular social group and concern with some novel questions (such as the symbolic and ritualized dimensions of protests, which for a host of reasons seemed particularly significant where Chinese students, a group lacking in economic clout, were concerned). And I immersed myself in secondary materials to which previously I had not paid much attention (the relatively limited number of previous studies of Chinese student activism) or been completely unaware of (the vast social science literature on 1960s American and European campus unrest).

By this point, I had a wide variety of works that provided partial models for the dissertation I actually needed to sit down and start writing. I began to envision a thesis that would begin with a scene-setting chapter, introducing readers to the city of Shanghai and the place of students within it, that owed something to the opening of Honig's book. I would need, after this, some narrative chapters, which could be a bit like those in John Israel's pioneering book on Chinese student movements. But interspersed with these I decided to insert some thematic chapters that explored particular topics (patterns of mobilization, the ritual and symbolic side of protests, and so forth), making for a kind of a book-within-a-book that owed more, structurally (and sometimes also theoretically), to Natalie Davis's first book and a couple of Charles Tilly's books that move between history and sociology in analyzing collective action.

Having moved back into Confucian territory with these new models to emulate, which between them provided me with a unique structure for a dissertation, I gave my inner Daoist free rein again. How? By allowing myself to start with whichever chapter I felt like writing (I think it was an analytic consideration of the always shifting but also repetitive repertoire of student protest tactics over the course of the first half of the twentieth century).

The same kind of Confucian-to-Daoist-to-Confucian-to-Daoist dialectic has served me well in other projects, though it never plays out quite the same way. I know that it won't work for everyone, but offer it here as one way to proceed—or at least something to think about as a partial model for emulation, some elements of which can be embraced, others discarded, as you delve into the dissertation.

8

APPROACHING THE ARCHIVES

By Jana Bouck Remy

While writing my dissertation prospectus and feeling "stuck" on how to connect my ideas with available archival resources, I asked Laurel Thatcher Ulrich for advice. She encouraged moving quickly from writing about what I hoped to do with my research and getting into the primary sources. She said, "Serendipity seldom strikes in the shower or on the beach. ... Serendipity most often happens in the archives."

In my experience, Ulrich's advice holds true. It's typically when I dedicate long hours to working in archival materials that I sort through the challenging points in my research: such insights rarely happen while I'm sitting on my couch.

However, one can't head for the archives without some planning and focus. Like the danger of going grocery shopping without a list—you might come home and realize that you've forgotten the most important ingredients for your recipes—successful historical sleuthing comes from being well organized and well prepared for your research trips. As such, I offer five steps that will aid in preparing for archival work.

BE REALISTIC

As you plan your project, consider how long it will take to gather the information that you're seeking—will it take months of tedious transcription from census records or involve travel to prohibitively expensive locales? Will it be a project that will continue to hold your interest even when you are homesick, stomach-sick, and you've been mugged for the second time while riding the bus to the courthouse? Will extended research trips be impractical because of family obligations or funding issues?

Because of the expense of research travel, it's important to confirm whether a trip to a distant archives is actually necessary. Check with your local libraries to find if your sources, such as periodicals, are available on microfiche or whether rare books might be available via interlibrary loan.

To get a reality check on your project, you should consult with your advisor and other scholars who've conducted a study similar to yours: inquire about their time frame and the efforts it took to procure the necessary data for their research. Make sure to ask what advice they have for researchers who are following in their footsteps. And plan accordingly.

ASK QUESTIONS

I'll repeat that well-worn aphorism that you've probably heard since kindergarten, "There's no such thing as a stupid question." As graduate students we aim to appear polished and prepared when we interact with archivists, librarians, and curators, so we might feel reticent to ask "stupid questions." However, given that we have a limited span of time for research trips (and limited funds), asking the right questions of the right people can increase efficiency and decrease frustration. Salient questions might range from inquiring about the policies of the research facility (Will you need a letter of introduction? Do they charge an entry fee? Will they allow laptop computers? Are they closed during the summer?) to inquiring about the specifics of the records you use (Is there a finding aid? What types of information are listed on a particular government form? What is the condition and legibility of the sources?).

Before a research trip I contact the relevant archivists, explaining my research objectives and asking for pointers in working at their facilities (of course, it goes without saying that you should do as much of your own legwork as possible before approaching the archivists—save your questions for those that aren't already answered on their web sites). When possible, I schedule an appointment to meet with the archivist when I first arrive at a facility, because I've found that he or she typically can point me to resources or records to augment those that I originally intended to peruse. Archivists are also helpful in answering detailed questions about institutional policies and procedures, which can speed along the first few frustrating days when working at an unfamiliar institution. For example, you'll want to ask whether they allow laptops, copying, or digital photography. If you intend to copy materials, be sure to know the policies beforehand so you don't have any unpleasant surprises when you receive your bill or when you realize that you've just run out of coins and there's nowhere nearby to make change.

CONSULT WITH OTHER SCHOLARS

This overlaps a bit with my last point but nevertheless warrants emphasis. Speaking to others who have worked in the archives can give you details such as the availability of the materials, external factors such as holiday schedules (there's nothing worse than planning a trip to an archives and then learning that it's closed the only week you're in town), and navigating challenging working situations. And, of course, by speaking to others who have worked in those same records you can make sure that your trip will be worth the trouble and expense.

Oftentimes when I'm doing archival work I'll strike up a conversation with other researchers. Though I rarely find that we have similar projects, there's a comforting collegiality in chatting with another scholar. Archival work can be terribly lonely—particularly when you're in an unfamiliar city and you return each evening to a dodgy hotel room. Maintaining a rigid research routine for days on end cannot only be isolating, but it can also be counterproductive to generating original thought. Talking about your project with another scholar can help you to clarify and make connections that you may not have seen before, and will help to give perspective to the detailed minutiae that is typical of archival inquiry.

HAVE A CONTINGENCY PLAN

When heading out on an archives visit, I create a list of prioritized action items. Typically it includes a list of the must-see sources I intend to consult, along with the necessary bibliographic details. In addition, I make a second list of items that I could consult in my spare time. For example, on a recent trip I intended to work solely in the manuscript holdings of a large public library. But I also knew that the regional historical society was nearby and had that on my second list of possible places to visit. After moving through the sources at the library much faster than I expected, I sought out the historical society and discovered that their holdings were also helpful to my project.

A wise colleague told me to plan at least three ways to approach a research question to prevent disappointment and frustration. If, for example, you intended to depend on court records for your data and then arrive at your municipal archives only to find that the cache of records had been lost in a recent fire, you know that you can then turn to plantation records, or whatever else you had listed as your second and third source possibilities.

Of course it might not be a natural disaster that destroyed your records, but you may simply find that the collection was neither as comprehensive nor as illuminating as you had hoped. Or perhaps you thought that you would need to sort through dozens upon dozens of boxes of military files to gather data for your work, and then discover that examining the soldiers' letters is a far more efficient way to gain the information that you're seeking.

BE TRUE TO YOUR SOURCES

Once you've asked all the right questions, procured the appropriate records, and jumped head first into the research process, you might find that the information doesn't support your thesis, or that it leads you on a tangent away from your original plan. This is to be expected. Your sources will reveal patterns and processes that weren't evident as you did your preliminary legwork in choosing your research topic. Being open to what you find in the archives will prevent the frustration of not finding what you were seeking. As Ulrich stated, it's important to remember that serendipitous encounters with records will allow you to think of your project in a new way. Thinking about what you will find in the archives is important, as is planning for it. But actually finding materials and then grappling to understand their significance and relevance—that is the business of historical research.

ASK QUESTIONS, REDUX

I'll now return to my earlier point about asking questions. As you're reading your primary sources, ask questions of the records and of yourself. I tend to keep either a small notebook or a file on my computer open while I'm researching and in which I write questions, puzzlements, and oddities. For example, in a recent project where I was reading a diary, a female writer constantly mentioned sewing *chemiloons*. What was this mysterious item? I wondered, and noted it in my questions log (I found out later that it's a type of underwear). Sometimes I want to note a question that's far larger than an unusual word; it will deal with contextualizing the social environment of a document, such as understanding the political instability following a particular election that may be affecting the life of my subjects in a way that I hadn't considered previously. So I will add a note to myself to learn more about that election and then ponder the ways in which it is relevant to my work.

During a research trip, at the end of each day I write some reflective thoughts to digest what I've examined and to give me some action items for my next day's work. I record these thoughts on a private blog, but others may choose to write in a notebook. The reflective practice of journaling keeps me focused on the larger issues at hand, and puts my daily discoveries into perspective. Because of this reflective process I may find new themes emerging, or I discover that I'm ready to direct my efforts towards another chapter or along a new line of inquiry.

As part of the reflective process, if time permits, it's important to spend time writing about the portions of your research that are relevant to your archival work. For example, if you find yourself commuting on a train each day, you may want to use that time for writing up a few paragraphs. Or set aside some time in the evenings after the archives closes. One colleague, who researches in an area where she could stay with relatives, told me that she opts for a hotel so she has the solitude to write in the evenings. If the time isn't available while you're actually on a research trip, you should plan ample time afterwards to write.

Depending on the nature of the sources, archival experiences will vary so widely that it's difficult to distill firm rules that will work for every project. Some of you will work in an esteemed institution with book-lined walls and codified procedures; others may be researching in areas where personal health and safety dictate the speed with which you can accomplish your research goals. Whatever your circumstances, your work in the archives will challenge you as a scholar, offering a variety of disappointments as well as the satisfaction of solving thorny historical mysteries. Preparing well for your archival work will reduce the frustration and increase the serendipities.

9

THINKING ABOUT SOURCES: PRIMARY AND SECONDARY DOCUMENTS

By Mary Lindemann

Historians who have reached the stage of writing a dissertation are familiar with the basic distinctions between primary and secondary sources. Roughly speaking, primary sources are documents created at the time and secondary sources are those that describe past events or processes and offer interpretations or analyses of them. Obviously, we are also all aware that the boundaries dividing primary from secondary sources are fluid; one era's secondary source may well be the primary source for a later period. Antiquarian literature (such as chronicles and family histories) often uncomfortably straddles the nominal categories of primary materials and secondary literature, but can be exceedingly valuable for providing obscure information or untangling historical conundrums. In either case, scholars must approach all sources critically and warily, querying each as to its creation, purpose, author(s), intent, and, especially, representativeness. For most students beginning their dissertations, uncertainties about primary and secondary sources and their appropriate uses, however, are rather different ones. The questions boil down to the relative weight one should place on primary and secondary materials and on how much influence each should exert. This seemingly simple problem is in fact devilishly difficult for most of us to negotiate with confidence.

The importance an author assigns to primary or secondary sources has more than a little to do with the particular approach brought to bear on a subject. Personal preferences and scholarly strengths also play a role: some of us are archive rats, others prefer to work more exclusively with published sources, or to enter into the main current of historical debate by using available and well-known materials to revise standard interpretations. Nonetheless, senior scholars and the profession as a whole tend to judge a "young" historian on the ability to engage primary materials competently and creatively.

The first issue confronting the neophyte historian is how much background reading should be done before embarking on research. Obviously, one assumes that ABDs have already acquired a command of the general literature of their field(s) and have also done fairly extensive reading around their dissertation topics (while preparing a prospectus, for instance). Background reading in a more focused way for a dissertation familiarizes one with the specific *published* work done on related topics, but it also offers an excellent opportunity to identify promising sources. While it is indefensible to pillage another scholar's footnotes (especially those in a dissertation), it is perfectly legitimate to learn from the *kinds* of materials another has employed or to identify source collections and holdings. One should, of course, also read such secondary material with an eye to the current historiography of a field and the ways in which arguments are crafted. Careful preparatory reading generates the essential background for framing reasonable, significant, and "do-able" research topics. Yet dangers lurk here as well. It is all too easy to be strongly influenced by previous work to the point that your contribution becomes derivative. Of course, you should not reinvent the wheel or embarrass yourself by demonstrating ignorance of current scholarship. Nor should you hesitate to acknowledge what others have accomplished. If someone has already used "your" sources, admit that and then explain where your handling of them differs. Keep in mind, however, that the most successful dissertations are not those that replicate someone else's topic, perhaps for another time or place, but which advance or challenge the current historiography by exploiting new materials or using older ones in a novel manner.

Much secondary reading, of course, *precedes* research. But it is equally critical to continue secondary reading *during* the research process itself. Research in primary materials should—and invariably will—raise questions that one had not previously considered or that even extensive reading in secondary literature has not suggested. It then often becomes necessary to take a break from the sources and read additionally to bolster your understanding of broader contexts and to clarify new insights. Finally, you will also want to continue secondary reading while actually writing. Here in particular, however, one must be careful to be instructed by this literature but not unduly swayed. Researchers should avoid slavishly following every new seductive idea that comes along. One must likewise be careful not to succumb to the temptation to create an interpretive pastiche that uses multiple and not always reconcilable ideas and approaches in an ill-advised attempt to be innovative or "thorough." Trust your primary sources and use them to control tendencies to fiddle with a framework you have conscientiously constructed. In short, let secondary material work for you, but don't be controlled by it. The greatest mark of a good historian is the ability to be creative, to craft robust interpretations, to uncover and exploit novel materials, or to forge new associations.

Thus, it is vital to let the documents (in whatever form) guide the research process. No one enters the archive as a *tabula rasa*. No professional historian is ever that naive. While there is much to recommend empiricism, history is, after all, primarily an interpretive endeavor. You need to frame cogent and pertinent research questions. Yet crossing the threshold into the archive laden with too many preconceived notions and theories to prove or disprove destroys much of the ability to learn from the documentation you find, to perceive which historical issues animated contemporaries, and to work out your own agenda.

Research in primary sources encompasses a variety of interventions. Obviously, the most traditional form is archival research, but sources come in many sizes, shapes, and descriptions. There are those sources composed to persuade, record, or take a position and these include written documents (chronicles, memoirs, diaries, inscriptions, and the like) and oral ones (ballads, recordings, tales, and so on). Additionally important are public documents; business, family, and personal records; customs; tools and artifacts; and even human remains. Each source, of course, requires the application of a particular skill in order to negotiate its complexities and force it to yield up its riches. Still, some general rules and caveats hold true for all. While this is not the place for an extensive discussion of how to use documents, some basics can be quickly stated. Whatever the source, the historian must probe its construction and pedigree. The number and kind of questions that address the transparency of the document (in whatever form) are infinite. Simple issues such as the purpose for which it was intended, the author, and the ways in which it was transmitted or stored must be addressed thoroughly. Yet although skepticism is the cardinal virtue of a practicing historian, one cannot allow questioning to degenerate into nihilism. To admit the problems or quirks of a source does not invalidate its use. In the end, all evidence is fragmentary and deceptive and *none* is fully believable. But your training as a historian and your willingness to interrogate your sources rigorously and honestly should bring you through to a *historical* understanding, even if an ultimate *truth* may always elude you. Ambiguities and uncertainties can also be turned to advantage, as can dissemblances and distortions that often reveal, for example, the terms of a debate, the discourses involved, or the varying points of view represented. In other words, doubt, but do not allow doubts to incapacitate you or force you into unnecessarily qualifying every statement. At some point you just have to get on with it!

The Internet has certainly changed how all of us do research. It facilitates the identification of primary materials and archival collections, and often even makes them accessible from the comfort of your study. It has dramatically increased our ability to prepare for research long before we open the first document box, turn the first manuscript page, or activate our tape recorder. Still, do not think that the Internet has all, or even most, of the answers and that its admittedly great possibilities and convenience obviate or reduce the need for on-the-spot research. In the process of learning the structure of an archive or other source depository, you will locate sources of whose existence you had no clue and these can make critical differences in your research. Thus, it is very important not to consider archival or primary research as mechanical or just an extended shopping trip to assemble the ingredients one needs to do the creative work of writing the dissertation. The best research is simultaneously creative and interactive. Spending more, rather than less, time in the archives will pay rich dividends not only in achieving the immediate goal—a well-researched dissertation—but also in identifying future viable topics.

The mass of materials a historian discovers is often intimidating and can prove to be a blessing and a curse. For the neophyte researcher—the dissertation writer—it is probably easiest to select a topic that relies on a clearly defined and deep cache of primary materials, such as the records of an orphanage, a government agency, a business, or a guild, or a massive collection of private papers and correspondence. These will often be contained in one or more archival "runs." Of course, some extremely innovative and highly impressive work has been done by historians who managed to pull together immense amounts of fascinating material from widely disparate, difficult, or obscure sources. But this is a tough job for a beginner. At the very worst, if you exploit a dense amount of material from one discrete source base, you may end up with a source-driven dissertation, but you will also—at the very least—have materials on which to build your monograph. And, after all, source-driven is always better than source-poor. Remember a dissertation is only the first step on the road to more substantial scholarly contributions: books and articles.

Finally, you need to decide when to stop your research, to gauge the point when you have adequately exploited your primary and secondary sources. This is a ticklish question. A useful technique is to take stock of your progress at regular intervals. You should frequently sit down and think about what you have accomplished and about whether your original plan of research is working out or whether you need to modify it in light of what you have discovered. You also need to be quite strict with yourself in addressing the question: do I have enough materials—and the right ones—to support the assertions that I want to make, to sustain my interpretation, and to make my points? Along the same lines, do not neglect contradictory or counter-vailing evidence. In fact, seek it out tenaciously. No case is airtight and you will inevitably weaken (rather than strengthen) your position by ignoring problems and dissonances in the documentation. In this respect, it probably helps to draft a fairly elaborate chapter outline about, say, midway in your research and then fill in the blanks by listing the materials you have to handle each point and assessing whether they are sufficient. This process may lead you to jettison some sections or even chapters, develop new ones, or—more usually—redraft several times what you started with. This is a natural and beneficial process and should be regarded as progress and not bemoaned as lamentably necessary retrenchment or back-filling. Research can be hard work and more than just occasionally frustrating, but most historians also find it fascinating and rewarding and, for some of us, it is our very *raison d'être*.

10

FROM NOTES TO NARRATIVE: FINDING THE STORY

By Deborah E. Harkness

Today, you are going to write. You sit at your desk, surrounded by stacks of books, piles of index cards, an outline for Chapter One that came to you in Starbucks and is written on a napkin, sharp number two pencils, different colors of post-it notes, one blank yellow notepad, a steaming cup of coffee, and your computer. Two hours later you are sitting exactly where you began. The only thing that has changed is that the coffee is gone. Not a single sentence floated through your brain and into your fingers in 120 minutes, you have had no paradigmatic breakthroughs, and you certainly cannot proclaim the morning's exercise in "writing" a success. You turn off your computer and leave the scene.

Every historian has days like this, even the most productive. Sometimes the words do not come easily or at all. What you need to do in these cases is to reconnect to the story that you want to tell. In 1895 the French author Jules Renard jotted down the following in his diary: "The story I am writing exists, written in absolutely perfect fashion, some place, in the air. All I must do is find it, and copy it." How do you move from the notes you have taken and the *plans* you have made and begin to actually *write* by finding the story that is lurking somewhere between your research, argument, historiography, and bibliography? It may seem to some that I am focusing too much on the work of the writer—and perhaps worse, the work of a writer of fiction—but I believe that the work of the historian and the writer are intertwined.

The reason why history and writing are tangled together is because, at the most basic level, all historians are storytellers. We come from a long lineage of epic poets, chroniclers, and bards. Despite this illustrious family tree it is all too easy, when faced with considerable professional pressures, to focus all our energy on research, argumentation, and historiography. It is true that no excellent work of history can fall short in any of these areas. At the same time, however, no excellent work of history can simply report findings, recount the arguments made by others, and expect to add a unique contribution to the mix. What distinguishes a good work of history from a great work are the stories a historian pieces together. Without a story, your writing experience can become mechanical and heavy, without human warmth or interesting plot twists and turns. What's worse, such writing can make the task of reading dull and uninspiring.

This is not, I think, what any of us wishes for when we set out to write. With so many other matters of concern on a historian's mind—accuracy, originality, and clarity, to name a few—perhaps failing to tell a good story can be considered a forgivable oversight. Nathaniel Hawthorne is reputed to have said, "Easy reading is damn hard writing." But it is only through the act of hard writing that we truly come to terms with the marvelous complexity of history and are forced to see the nuances in our evidence.

Happily, there is help for those of us interested in damn hard writing, and much of it comes from other writers—particularly writers of fiction. There is one book that I particularly recommend: Ann Lamott's bestselling *Bird by Bird: Some Instructions on Writing and Life.* In this inspiring book about the *process* of writing, Lamott gives struggling writers no magical cure-alls or false promises that everything is going to be easy and all right. She acknowledges that writing consumes your life, and that writing is never smooth but full of false starts and dead ends. And she talks openly and honestly about just how hard it is to find the story and tell it well.

My advice to you when setting out to write is to think like a *writer* and begin paying attention to two basic, yet crucial, elements: characters and plot. It is going to feel strange to briefly suspend your concerns for evidence, argument, and accuracy. But the most vital elements of any story well told are the characters. When you have a moment, jot down at least one central character in your dissertation or book. One day when you are stuck, go ahead and list them all, and keep updating the list as you find new characters and abandon old ones. Whenever you are mired down in your work you can always turn your attention away from the accusatory blinking cursor and towards writing up brief, one- or two-paragraph biographical sketches for each of them. At first, the sketches will read like bad entries in *Who's Who,* full of names and dates and places. But as you come to learn about your characters, you will be able to breathe more life into them. Knowing what someone liked for breakfast, who their neighbors were, and what books they owned will lead in ways you cannot predict to a multi-dimensional sense of your research subjects. The final goal of collecting this information and writing up character sketches is to reach a point in writing where you stop *telling* your readers about a character in pages upon pages of descriptive prose and begin *showing* them using powerful images and the insights that come only after years of close companionship with your subjects.

Getting to know your characters depends on deep research in a wide variety of sources; it also depends on listening to them and asking the right kinds of questions. The most important thing to know about any character—and the hardest to figure out—is what matters most to them. Lamott in *Bird by Bird* again offers help to historians by asking writers to uncover and then articulate "what each character cares most about in the world because then you will have discovered what's at stake" in the story that you are trying to tell. The question of what is at stake is the great bugaboo of historical writing and argumentation. Figuring out what's most important to one or all of your main characters brings clarity to your argument, gives structure your dissertation, and helps you to find the story.

Of course, not all historians are telling stories primarily about humans. I think that Lamott's advice is useful even if you are working with inanimate objects and numbers—although I suspect there are still some human beings wandering through the rooms full of steam engines and demographic data that you have collected. One possibility for such cases is that you can ask yourself what is most important *about* your steam engine. Is it where it was made? What about who made it, or who owns it, or where they bought it? Knowing the answers is as important—perhaps even more important— when some of your characters are cities, steam engines, and trees as when they are poets, parlor maids, or public librarians.

There are times when, to your horror, the "main" characters turn out to occupy minor roles in your story. It is easy when you begin to assume the main characters are the people you have heard of before and already know something about, thanks to the work of other historians. When writing about Elizabethan natural history, for example, I naturally assumed that the period's most famous botanist would be the main character in my story. I tried everything I could to keep him in the spotlight, but try as I might he kept getting upstaged by apothecaries and silk merchants no one knew much about. Trust me, this is a good thing. Who wants to hear a story that only contains familiar characters? Be courageous, and if you think Hawthorne's neighbor's cousin's gardener is a main character, stick with it and see what happens. You might surprise yourself—and the rest of us—by being right.

As you develop your characters, you will find connections between them that you never imagined. A fiction writer like Anne Lamott would tell you that this is the moment when you see the first glimmers of your story's plot. The relationships among the main characters create the narrative arc or plot for a work of fiction—and it does for a work of history, too. A useful formula for developing plots and subplots is described by Lamott in *Bird by Bird* as "setup, buildup, and payoff." The setup that most historians use—and sometimes overuse—is the telling anecdote. In the setup we are introduced to main characters and to the time period, place, and scope of the plot. For historians, the buildup includes the unfolding of subplots and the subarguments that they are associated with, the use of evidence to substantiate arguments, and the exploration of characters to show us what's at stake. Finally, in any great work of history there is the payoff— that moment in a book when the pieces fall into place and you find yourself agreeing with the author's claims about what is at stake. For most readers, the payoff of a great work of history is transformative, and we will never look at the major characters in the same way again.

By getting to know your characters and following the plot as it unfolds through relationships your characters have with each other, you will find the story that you are trying to tell. But finding the story, Anne Lamott warns us, "will often take place in fits and starts." "Don't worry about it," she counsels. Just "keep trying to move the story forward. There will be time later to render it in a smooth and seamless way." Let your characters surprise you, and let the plot unfold in ways you do not expect. To write is to accept that every word will change, that the story will be ornery, and that characters will refuse to behave.

We are, all of us, writers. Often, however, we confuse what E. L. Doctorow called "planning to write"—the "outlining ... researching ... talking to people about what you're doing"—with actual writing. Doctorow clearly distinguished planning to write from writing. And it can be helpful for us to remember that distinction, too, or we are likely to remain stuck in the hunting and gathering stage of project development, endlessly returning to our notes and our archives without a word to show for it. We do so because we are frightened by the enormous task before us, and we do so because the voices of our inner critics are so loud. But we also keep piling up books and filling out index cards because we have become so overwhelmed with information that we have lost the story, and can no longer find the main characters with two hands and a flashlight.

Finding the story is a challenging task, and writing that story down and doing justice to it is even more difficult. I've suggested here that thinking about character and plot is one way to find the story and tell it in a convincing and lively fashion. Nothing I have said is meant to substitute for the meticulous research, structured argumentation, and scrupulous reviews of the scholarly literature you have been trained to do. Instead, finding the story and then telling it well adds something to your existing, hard-won historical skills. In the very near future you will find yourself sitting in front of paper, typewriter, or computer. You will be trying to write. You may even be planning to write and thus armed with outlines, notes, and coffee. I hope that if you get that far, you will focus on your main characters, follow them as the plot unfolds, and begin to actually *write*.

11

WHEN WORDS DON'T COME ...

By James J. Sheehan

Are there any writers who don't sometimes fear that the words won't come, that the page will remain blank, the computer screen empty? In *A Moveable Feast*, Ernest Hemingway describes how, as a young writer, he dealt with this fear: "I would stand and look out over the roofs of Paris and think, 'Do not worry. You have always written before and you will write now. All you have to do is write one true sentence. Write the truest sentence you know.'" While most of us do not have the roofs of Paris outside our windows to inspire us, we can all take heart from the fact that we have written before and that we can all try to write one true sentence, by which Hemingway meant a simple, declarative sentence—straightforward, unadorned, and as clear and precise it can possibly be.

Unlike Hemingway and other creative writers, we historians do not have to make up the one true sentence.

Because we do not have to find the words to transform our emotions or experience into prose, writing history is easier than writing fiction. But we do have to find the words that express what we know—more frequently, what we have recently learned—about the past. Our problem, therefore, is to craft sentences, paragraphs, chapters, and eventually books that will make sense out of the broken mosaic of information that we have gathered from our sources. The fiction writer's challenge is to create; the historian's is to define and organize.

For us, the true sentence that can help us make the words come (or return) should be an answer to a deceptively simple question: What is this (paragraph, chapter, dissertation, book) really about? I am convinced that writing problems are almost always thinking problems in disguise. The words aren't the problem; we have lots and lots of them, often more than we need. If we know what we want to say, we can find the right words to say it. However, if we start to write without knowing what we want to say (or, as more often happens, wrongly thinking we know) the result will be that all too familiar sort of stylistic wheel spinning that digs us deeper and deeper into the mud of authorial frustration and produces eventual immobility.

Knowing what we want to say requires deciding what our subject really is. First and foremost, this means determining how the story begins and ends. If we are lucky, this will be a question of chronology; answering it will always shape everything else. Always remember: narrative is your friend. The second issue requires us to make the critical distinction between subject and context, that is, between what is central and what is peripheral, what gets kept and—hardest of all—what gets left out. As we know, everything is connected to everything else, but there is not room for everything in any single work. (You should assume that in any given project you will end up excluding some of your favorite facts, quotations, and incidents—painful but necessary sacrifices for the good of the whole.)

There is a crude but simple test for whether you have solved these two problems: can you come up with accurate titles for the project as a whole and for its most important parts? Of course, the title of the project will change as you learn more about it, but that is all the more reason to keep defining and redefining it. I am always surprised when, after having worked on a project for weeks, sometimes months, students fall silent when I ask them for a title. In my experience, this silence is frequently one of the warning signs of writing problems.

I am also convinced that outlines can help us to determine the shape and content of our story. I know excellent historians who never outline; they find their story by the act of writing itself. But for me, an outline is a necessary step, or rather a series of necessary steps in the writing process. I use outlines from the start of a project to sketch its preliminary shape. Then I use them to make an inventory of the material I have gathered—the larger the project, the more necessary I find this to be. One way of starting this inventory process is to see if I can divide my material into three (perhaps two, never more than five) parts (each, of course, with a tentative title) and then each of these into three. At this point, some material—usually gathered at the beginning of the project—will not fit and can be set aside. Obviously if too much gets set aside, there is something wrong. Sometimes (and this has happened to me more than once) it is because I was trying to tell two stories rather than one. If so, then I had to decide which one to tell first. It also usually becomes clear that there is too much material on some aspects of the story and not enough on others. Now is the time to ask, does this mean that the shape of the story should change or that it is necessary to go back to the sources?

The outline as inventory slowly evolves into the outline as blueprint, that is, the outline becomes a guide to how the project can be constructed from the materials at hand. For an outline to be useful it must be tentative, constantly revised as you go on. That is, indeed, one of the outline's great merits; it is much easier to produce and therefore much easier to alter than pages of prose. But that is also one of the outline's dangers: it can conceal serious problems of organization and transition. It is important, therefore, not to allow the outline to become an end in itself. Like Hegel's owl of Minerva, the best outline will appear at dusk, after it is too late; that is, after the problems of writing have been resolved. The only way to test an outline's robustness is by starting to write.

Where to begin? In my opinion, there is only one answer to that question: at the beginning. Every writer, at one time or another, is tempted to begin somewhere else. Since Chapter Three, we try to convince ourselves, will be an especially easy (or difficult or interesting or convenient) chapter, we should start there. In my own painful experience, this has always been a mistake. The Chapter Three that then gets written first is usually not Chapter Three at all, since it does not follow from the yet to be written Chapters One and Two. Once Chapters One and Two are written, Chapter Three will either end up being rewritten, and thereby taking much longer than if it had been done in order, or discarded completely.

In writing, as in chess, the opening moves are critically important. This is true of the work as a whole and of its individual parts. The opening is, of course, important for the readers because it will encourage them to read on and prepare them to understand what follows. But the opening is equally important for the author because it establishes the trajectory of the paragraph, chapter, and book. Here, too, the author must be prepared to sacrifice the precious detail for the good of the whole: the witty quotation or striking anecdote that we love so much may not be what we need to start our story. Some of the best introductions I have ever written had to be discarded since they were not, alas, good introductions to the work at hand.

If writing problems are essentially problems of definition and organization, then the writing should get easier as a work progresses; the shape of the story becomes better defined and the amount of material to be mastered decreases. If this does not happen, if writing becomes harder rather than easier, then it is time to step back and be sure that you have really solved the key questions of definition and organization. Sometimes simple changes in the location of a chapter or a section can make things flow again. Here is where a friendly reader can often be of great assistance. The important thing is not to give up. It is almost always more difficult to begin writing again after a long delay than to press on.

Writing problems are more common at the beginning of a project, but they can occur at any time. For most of us, writing is hard work even if the best writers can make it look easy. (If it doesn't look easy, Fred Astaire once said about dancing, you aren't working hard enough.) Writing—or at least writing history—is a demanding, difficult, and often frustrating craft, but it is a craft that can be mastered by everyone reading these lines. As Hemingway wrote, knowing that we have written before and will write again is an essential source of courage and consolation on those occasions when words don't come.

12

Towards a Unified Document: The Big Picture in Dissertation Writing

By Lary May

At the height of Stanley Kubrick's career, an interviewer asked the great film director how he made such classic works as *Dr. Strangelove* and *2001*. After a brief pause Kubrick answered that first came the emotional inspiration, followed by discipline and hard work to make that inspiration a reality. The inspiration for Kubrick was the "big story" or theme that had to make sense of the many things that compose film making: plot details, the visual images, the performances, and even the distribution of the final product. Having worked in both mediums, as a scholar and movie producer's assistant, it seems to me that Kubrick's insight provides an apt metaphor for the process of writing a doctoral dissertation. With my own experience in mind, I remind students that writing the doctoral dissertation culminates one's metamorphosis from a passive absorber of others' ideas to the creator of original scholarship. The dissertation is the first of many projects in a scholar's career, but since it has to engage one's interest over a long period of time, the conceptual framework that provides a unified document is critical to the task.

In the process of creating the dissertation, the student will have gathered from libraries and other sources hundreds of research materials. The various notes and sources, however, have to be organized around a conceptual framework that gives cohesion to the whole. In other words, once the topic has been chosen and the advisor and writer agree that the dissertation will make an original contribution to historical scholarship, the framework or the "inspiration" that has been implicit in the work must come into focus, serving as the means to organize the data into a cohesive argument. Learning this task will allow one to finish the project and also provide a major learning skill that will be used repeatedly in one's future career.

So how can we learn this skill? Let me illustrate this issue with a telling example. I once had the privilege of guiding the thesis of a very talented student. After two years of research, he presented me with the first three chapters of his thesis. These chapters were well written, complete with a rich insights and original materials. Yet the limitation of this first effort was that the chapters were all background without a foreground. The first difficulty was an overabundance of historical detail; events and people appeared without a rationale for their importance. The writer in many ways was "too close" to his project. He had assumed that the reader understood exactly what was important about the topic, and how the material he presented in vivid detail altered previous modes of understanding. Though the vivid evidence did stimulate great interest, an overarching theme that would answer the question of "so what" was absent. In other words, the material was "interesting" but it lacked the big picture that would explain the project's importance to the lay reader and professional historian alike.

One way to answer the "so what" question is to open the thesis with an introductory anecdote or a "hook." I often illustrate this point by explaining to students that long before I found my "calling" as a historian, I worked for a film producer at Universal Pictures in the "swinging" London of the 1960s. In addition to making coffee and running errands for my employer, I worked to organize the producer's current script that would go into production within the year. I tried in particular to create opening scenes that "grabbed" the audience by the lapels so that they would be entertained and introduced to the film's larger theme. The opening scene was expected to frame the "big story" that was to inform the narrative and action that was to follow. Above all the viewer need to be "hooked" into our story.

Though the mediums and audiences for film and historical writing are very different, I have found it possible to transfer many of the lessons I learned in constructing the big picture in films to the art of writing history. A classic example of a great "hook" can be found in the opening pages of Godfrey Hodgson's *America in Our Time*. Hodgson's organizing theme is that in the wake of World War II, Americans created in politics a new ideology of liberal consensus. Political leaders assumed that economic growth would create a middle-class society to which all citizens could assimilate without class or racial conflict. But by the 1960s experiences that would not "fit" the consensus shattered that liberal ethos. To introduce readers to that theme, Hodgson contrasts two of the major presidential inaugural speeches that began and ended the decade. In 1960 President John Kennedy asserted that America at home was a harmonious society, while the nation's only danger lay in foreign affairs. Eight years later President Richard Nixon claimed that the nation's perils came not from abroad, but from the home front. Why did war protests, a youthful counterculture, and the black revolt shatter the Cold War consensus? After his big picture came into view with these two events, Hodgson then went on to address these questions in the book itself.

While Hodgson had a clear framework for his study, most dissertation writers do not have such a clear organizing principle in mind when they first begin their projects. In searching for that big story, I encourage students first to put the project in perspective as they gather new materials. By the time they have started their research, in other words, most thesis writers have mastered the historical literature and are aware of the unresolved questions in their field. It is important to realize that the doctoral thesis will answer some of those questions, but it cannot resolve them all. I encourage students to facilitate this process by keeping a journal while they do research and write the dissertation. Here they can jot down ideas that can later be used to form the project's big idea, or for other projects in the future. I have also found it worthwhile to record ideas that arrive at strange times, such as those that come to one in that twilight zone between sleep and wakefulness in the morning.

To begin to bring these fragmentary insights into the larger conceptual framework, I suggest that students begin to organize their materials around the themes recorded in the journal. One might begin this process by composing a three-part introduction with sections that address the three main parts of the thesis: the what, why, and how of the larger project. The "what" is the subject of the thesis; the "why" is the larger question it poses for current knowledge; and the "how" revolves around the methods and the big story that will bring the materials into a unified theme. Over the years, I have found that graduate students often neglect one or another of these parts to the detriment of the whole. At first, the student I described earlier went into elaborate detail in explaining the historiography, methods, and theories of his thesis. Lost in the discussion were the central question that would be addressed and the organizing themes that would drive the story forward.

Once the "big picture" has come into focus, the issue becomes how to organize a large body of research into single and multiple chapters that tell the larger story. As the organizing strategy comes into view, it is critical to avoid what one might call the one-thing-after-another narrative. Facts do not speak for themselves. At key points in each chapter, one needs to remind the reader of the underlying analysis that propels the story, and how that analysis advances in a fresh way the overall theme. Within each chapter, as the narrative unfolds, the writer must choose where and how to interrupt the flow of the story with comments that move the analysis onto a new plane. As in a detective story or film, this analytical strategy brings out the meaning lying beneath the events and the writer's interpretation or explanation of those facts.

There are several ways to accomplish this task in each chapter. A brief foreshadowing of the big story can be placed at the start of each chapter and the analysis can be interjected at key points in the narrative. Or the larger implications of the discussion can be added at the end in the chapter's conclusion. Two examples of this back-ended mode appear in Lawrence Levine's essay "William Shakespeare and the American People: A Study in Cultural Transformation" in *The Unpredictable Past: Explorations in American Cultural History* and in George Lipsitz's fine essay "The Meaning of Memory: Family, Class, and Ethnicity in Early Network Television" in his *Time Passages: Collective Memory and American Popular Culture*. Both Levine and Lipsitz take the reader directly into their subjects, holding their larger analysis in abeyance, and suggesting only briefly the larger scholarly issues that are at stake. Only at the end of the chapter do they present an extended discussion of the larger implications of their findings for our understanding of American history.

Another closely related problem is where and how one creates from several distinct chapters a unified document. A common tendency for beginning writers is to treat each chapter as an isolated entity. With isolated chapters, the reader is also asked to "jump" into the topic, without telling the reader how the fresh material relates to the discussion that preceded it or how the new material advances the big story of the thesis as a whole. One way to overcome this difficulty is to organize the chapters in such a way that together they drive forward the big story. Within each chapter, it is also useful to provide the reader with guideposts that link the new discussion to a previous section, while alerting the reader how the material in the current section will alter the way we have previously understood the topic of the thesis. One method for accomplishing this unity is to use one of the opening paragraphs to link together the earlier parts, suggesting how the new section advances the thesis along new lines or plays the larger theme in a fresh key.

I have also found that both the advisor and other graduate students can help writers bring into focus the conceptual frame that will create a unified document. The value of the first is derived from my personal experience with my own mentor, Alexander Saxton in the history department at UCLA in the late 1960s and early 1970s. Periodically Saxton asked that I show him individual chapters as they were written. Since then I have supplemented this process with the creation of larger communal groups. Believing that graduate students, even after they have completed their coursework, should not work in isolation, I have encouraged dissertation writers to form groups to share their thoughts and work with others. A group of peers can provide an ideal venue for bringing "fresh eyes" to chapter drafts and help each other formulate the "big story" for their thesis. These groups either meet on their own or at my house on a monthly basis. All in all, I have found that writing the doctoral dissertation requires discipline, inspiration, and hard work, but it can yield as much satisfaction as a good movie.

13

THE FINAL RITES OF PASSAGE: SUBMITTING AND DEFENDING THE DISSERTATION

By **Thomas S. Mullaney**

From what I have gleaned through informal conversations, the process of submitting and defending one's dissertation was a far more complicated enterprise in the era before personal computing. This era (let's call it "B.P.C.") was a time of correction fluid and a steady wrist, when typos haunted the submission process like gremlins. Interstitial additions were even more onerous, requiring the retyping of entire sections, perhaps even entire chapters. For those who went through it, the write-up phase seems to have constituted something like a bonding experience. Like the orals process, it produced veterans, "war stories," and a community of commiseration.

In the era of personal computing, this angst-ridden dimension of the submission process has largely faded from collective consciousness. Printing in triplicate is effortless, typos are automatically detected by software dictionaries, and the insertion of content demands little more than a few keystrokes. In the worst-case scenario, additional content might require an author to adjust the starting page of subsequent chapters, but even this can be achieved through no more than four quick procedures: *View, Header and Footer, Format Page Number, Start at* x. For those using bibliographic software such as EndNote, the addition of new sources requires even fewer steps: *Tools, Format Bibliography*. The whole process is simple to the point of invisibility. As a consequence, hardly anyone talks about the process anymore.

Do not let technology fool you, however. The final stage of the dissertation remains today what it has always been: a rite of passage comprising a series of steps designed to bring your work into compliance with a body of work known as "dissertations." During this process, the files in your computer—paginated according to any number of different methods, checkered with "notes to self" regarding this or that missing citation, presented on the page in any number of different fonts, etc.—finally take shape.

As we review some of the primary steps of the submission process, I invite the reader to appreciate the ritualistic qualities of each—to think of them as more than technical and administrative minutiae. Pagination, for example, is much more than the act of assigning consecutive numbers to your dissertation chapters. For many authors, it is the first time they will see their dissertations as coherent texts containing sustained sets of arguments. Likewise, formatting is much more than the standardization of fonts and margins. It is the moment when, perhaps for the first time, the author will begin to see his or her work through the eyes of an outside reader.

With this preface, let us jump into the technical dimensions of the submission process.

SCHEDULING

Before plunging into the finer points of spacing, pagination, citation, and the like, the first and most important step you must take is to familiarize yourself thoroughly and accurately with the scheduling requirements of your home institution. In some cases, the process of final submission and defense requires the completion of official forms six months in advance. If you do not fill out all of these forms, at the right time, in the proper order, *you will not be able to submit or defend your thesis at the time you had planned.* To this end, the most important first step you can take is to visit your university's dissertation office and to review all the relevant deadlines. Some key dates include, but are not limited to, the submission of an intent-to-graduate form, the selection and official approval of your defense committee, scheduling an official defense date, circulation of the dissertation to your committee members, and the submission of the signed and completed dissertation for digitization and binding.

The larger significance of this process hardly requires explanation. This is the moment when you announce, both to yourself and to others, your intent to enter the final phase of the graduate program. It is the decision to leave the seclusion of the writing process—with all its solitude and self-structured time—and re-enter a world in which you must abide by a schedule set by others. For those about to take up a teaching position, this seclusion will never happen again.

PAGINATION

Page numbering is particularly important, and you should take care to follow the guidelines of your institution strictly. While variations exist, the following rules of thumb should guide you in determining which sections of your dissertation do and do not receive page numbers and, among those that do include page numbers, whether they should be considered as part of the prefatory or body pages. Often, the title page, the copyright page, and abstract pages are not assigned page numbers, and do not count towards the overall length of the dissertation. Following these are the prefatory pages, which are assigned a consecutive series of lower-case roman numerals. This applies to the table of contents, lists of charts and graphics, dedications, acknowledgements, and the preface (if you choose to write one). The body pages, which include all pages not listed above, are assigned consecutive numbers beginning with the number one. This applies to photographs, tables, graphs, bibliography, and appendices, as well.

Besides the fact that pagination needs to be undertaken with care, there is a larger significance to this within the submission process. If the reader is anything like me, what you refer to at dinner parties as your "dissertation," as a singular entity, is in fact a scattered collection of files on your hard drive written in an order other than the way they will appear in the final work. For each of these files, moreover, you probably have multiple versions, arranged within a makeshift hierarchy of nested folders. What is more, if you have presented your work, whether at conferences or in the form of book chapters or journal articles, your hard drive will likely contain multiple "final" versions of the same chapter. And let's not even talk about all the tables, charts, and undeveloped ideas that never made it into the final version. The point here is: your dissertation is not really a dissertation until all of its components have been brought into congruence with one another, whether in the form of a single word processing document or in a series of consecutively paginated files. More than anything else, the process of paginating all of your chapters is the final act of creating your dissertation. As simple as consecutive numbers are, there is nothing quite so illuminating as seeing how the conclusion of one chapter, marked "Page 72," connects to the intro of the next, marked "Page 73."

FORMATTING

According to regulations outlined by the graduate program web site of Princeton University, a dissertation "must show that the candidate has technical mastery of the field and is capable of doing independent research. This study must enlarge or modify current knowledge in a field or present a significant new interpretation of known materials." For the candidate in the early or middle stages of the dissertation process, such abstract requirements as this serve to guide, inspire, and terrify. "I am thoroughly versed in the literature of my field, but do I possess a 'technical mastery'?" "I consider my argument to be exciting and important, but is it new and significant?"

One benefit of the write-up phase is that such abstract definitions of the dissertation fade largely into the background. Faced with a set of rigid regulations and hard-and-fast deadlines, there is very little time to ruminate over whether one's dissertation is going to "enlarge or modify current knowledge." Instead, you must now worry about fonts, footnotes, paper quality, spacing, and so on. In this sense, the submission phase should come as a relief, as it momentarily neutralizes the forms of psychological stress that build up over the course of the writing phase, when the author is alone with his or her thoughts. These stresses will resurface later, of course, most notably during the job search process and while you prepare your book manuscript. But, for the meantime, you would do best to revel in the psychological release that comes when you concentrate the entirety of your focus on margins, spacing, font, and other technical matters. As the Zen saying goes: "When you're doing the dishes, do the dishes." With that in mind, let's review the basic formatting requirements. Again, these may vary according to your institution, so be sure to follow the specific instructions you receive.

Margins. The top, bottom, and right margins are fixed at the normal one-inch minimum. The left margin must leave additional room for binding.

Spacing. The text, abstract, dedication, acknowledgements, and table of contents are double-spaced. Block quotes (quotations of considerable length) are single-spaced and indented on both sides. Footnotes, endnotes, and bibliographic entries should be single-spaced with double spacing between each entry.

Font. Times New Roman, in twelve-point font, is typically the typeface of choice, although other standard fonts may also be acceptable.

Paper. You should double-check paper requirements with your home institution, but a general list of requirements for the final paper copy include acid-free, watermarked, pure white, 100 percent cotton bond, twenty or twenty-four pounds, standard 8.5x11 inch format. All pages should be printed single-sided.

Notes. Check with your advisor, as well as your institution's dissertation office, to determine the proper location of your notes. Normally, they are placed in one of three locations: at the bottom of each page (single-spaced, with space between each note), at the end of each chapter, or at the end of the dissertation (prior to the bibliography). You will also want to check on the preferred mode of in-text citation; some institutions permit the use of parenthetical references, while others require the use of footnotes or endnotes throughout.

CONCLUSION

By this point in the process, you are cloistered in one of three places: your home office, your graduate student lounge, or the computer lab at your home institution. You are standing close to the laser printer, and you are printing out a copy of your entire dissertation for the first time. By page two hundred, the printer is hot to the touch, and everyone in the room has grown accustomed to the whir of the cylinder. You remove the pages, fifteen or twenty at a time, and place them carefully atop the growing pile. You periodically tap the edges against the table, delighted to watch them disappear into a uniform brick of paper. In your chest is a mounting excitement and in your nostrils the intoxicating fragrance of toner. Quite literally, your dissertation is taking shape before your eyes. Take a moment to celebrate this accomplishment. It's done!

ABOUT THE AUTHORS

Leora Auslander teaches modern European social history at the University of Chicago, where she was the founding director of the Center for Gender Studies and the director of graduate studies in the history department for two years.

Before becoming William B. Umstead Professor of History at the University of North Carolina at Chapel Hill, **W. Fitzhugh Brundage** had enough job interviews over the years to acquire a long litany of mishaps. His area of specialization is the modern United States, especially the American South. His most recent book is *The Southern Past: A Clash of Race and Memory* (2005).

Anthony Grafton teaches the intellectual and cultural history of early modern Europe at Princeton University, where he has been since 1975. His books include *Joseph Scalinger, What Was History?* and *The Footnote: A Curious History*. From 2004 through 2007 he served as vice president of the AHA's Professional Division.

In nearly fifty years of graduate teaching at Case Western Reserve University, the University of Michigan, the University of California at Irvine, and Johns Hopkins University, **Jack P. Greene**, Andrew W. Mellon Professor in the Humanities Emeritus at Johns Hopkins, supervised eighty-seven completed doctoral dissertations, the most recent at Johns Hopkins in June 2008. He now lives in East Greenwich, Rhode Island, where he continues his lifelong quest to learn how to write history.

Deborah Harkness is professor of history at the University of Southern California. A historian of early modern science, she has written *John Dee's Conversations with Angels* and *The Jewel House: Elizabethan London and the Scientific Revolution*. She is currently at work on a book, *Living the Experimental Life in Early Modern Britain*, which explores the intersection of scientific, experimental, and domestic cultures in the seventeenth-century Anglo-American world. Her research and writing have received awards from agencies and organizations including the History of Science Society, the Renaissance Society of America, the Guggenheim Foundation, and the National Humanities Center.

Mary Lindemann is professor of history at the University of Miami. She is the author of four books: *Patriots and Paupers: Hamburg, 1712–1830* (1990); *Health and Healing in Early Modern Germany* (1996); *Medicine and Society in Early Modern Europe* (1999); and *Liaisons dangereuses: Sex, Law, and Diplomacy in the Age of Frederick the Great* (2006). She is currently preparing a second edition of *Medicine and Society* (due out in 2009 or 2010) and writing a book on political culture in three early modern cities: Amsterdam, Antwerp, and Hamburg.

Lary May is professor of American studies and history at the University of Minnesota. He received his PhD in American cultural history at UCLA in 1977, where his doctoral advisor was Alexander Saxton. He is the author of *Screening Out the Past: Hollywood and the Birth of Mass Culture* (1980); *Recasting America: Culture and Politics in the Age of Cold War* (1989); and *The Big Tomorrow: Hollywood and the Politics of the American Way* (2000). He is currently writing a new book tentatively entitled *Foreign Affairs: Global Hollywood and the Making of Postwar American Culture.*

Thomas S. Mullaney joined Stanford University in 2006 as assistant professor in modern Chinese history after completing his PhD at Columbia University. Mullaney's research examines the complex historical and sociological processes that connect the production of modern social scientific knowledge to the production of modern state power. His research deals with the role of the social sciences in the history of state and nation formation, ethnic and racial identity, state and social scientific practices of individual and collective identification, classification theory, and transnational and comparative world history.

Jana Remy is a PhD candidate in U.S. history at University of California at Irvine and is a current recipient of the Andrew V. White Scholarship from the UC Humanities Research Institute. Jana is frequently invited to speak about using web-based technologies in humanities research and she also founded the Making History Podcast (www.makinghistorypodcast.com).

Vanessa R. Schwartz is professor of history, art history, and film and directs the Visual Studies Graduate Certificate at the University of Southern California (USC). A historian on modern visual culture, she was trained in modern European history with a concentration on France and urban culture at Princeton (Phi Beta Kappa, 1986) and University of California at Berkeley where she received her PhD in 1993. She is currently writing *Modern France: A Very Short Introduction* (Oxford University Press) and has begun a new research project on the "jet age." Prof. Schwartz wishes to thank Nancy Troy and Karen Haltunnen of USC and Anne Higonnet, her Social Science Research Council Dissertation Proposal Development Fellowship research director, for their perspectives and advice on her chapter.

James Sheehan is Dickason Professor in the Humanities and professor emeritus of history at Stanford University. His most recent book is *Where Have All the Soldiers Gone? The Transformation of Modern Europe*, published in 2008. In 2005 he was president of the American Historical Association.

Jeffrey N. Wasserstrom is professor of history at the University of California at Irvine and the editor of the *Journal of Asian Studies*. He is the author, most recently, of *China's Brave New World—And Other Tales for Global Times* (Indiana University Press, 2007) and *Global Shanghai, 1850–2010: A History in Fragments* (Routledge, 2009). In addition to publishing in various academic periodicals, he has contributed to a wide range of general interest periodicals, including the *Times Literary Supplement* (London) and the *Los Angeles Times,* and he co-founded and regularly writes for The China Beat: Blogging How the East is Read (http://thechinabeat.blogspot.com/).